IF F

👤 _____

✉ _____

📱 _____

Greater Than a Tourist Book Series
Reviews from Readers

I think the series is wonderful and beneficial for tourists to get information before visiting the city.

-Seckin Zumbul, Izmir Turkey

I am a world traveler who has read many trip guides but this one really made a difference for me. I would call it a heartfelt creation of a local guide expert instead of just a guide.

-Susy, Isla Holbox, Mexico

New to the area like me, this is a must have!

-Joe, Bloomington, USA

This is a good series that gets down to it when looking for things to do at your destination without having to read a novel for just a few ideas.

-Rachel, Monterey, USA

Good information to have to plan my trip to this destination.

-Pennie Farrell, Mexico

Great ideas for a port day.

-Mary Martin USA

Aptly titled, you won't just be a tourist after reading this book. You'll be greater than a tourist!

-Alan Warner, Grand Rapids, USA

Even though I only have three days to spend in San Miguel in an upcoming visit, I will use the author's suggestions to guide some of my time there. An easy read - with chapters named to guide me in directions I want to go.

-Robert Catapano, USA

Great insights from a local perspective! Useful information and a very good value!

-Sarah, USA

This series provides an in-depth experience through the eyes of a local. Reading these series will help you to travel the city in with confidence and it'll make your journey a unique one.

-Andrew Teoh, Ipoh, Malaysia

>TOURIST

GREATER THAN A TOURIST – MACKINAC ISLAND MICHIGAN USA

50 Travel Tips from a Local

Jane Hughes

Greater Than a Tourist- Mackinac Island USA Copyright © 2018 by CZYK Publishing LLC. All Rights Reserved.

All rights reserved. No part of this book may be reproduced in any form or by any electronic or mechanical means including information storage and retrieval systems, without permission in writing from the author. The only exception is by a reviewer, who may quote short excerpts in a review.

Cover designed by: Ivana Stamenkovic
Cover Image: https://pixabay.com/en/mackinaw-mackinac-island-michigan-2650154/

CZYK Publishing Since 2011.

Greater Than a Tourist
Visit our website at www.GreaterThanaTourist.com

Lock Haven, PA
All rights reserved.
ISBN: 9781796883084

>TOURIST
50 TRAVEL TIPS FROM A LOCAL

\>TOURIST

BOOK DESCRIPTION

Are you excited about planning your next trip?

Do you want to try something new?

Would you like some guidance from a local?

If you answered yes to any of these questions, then this Greater Than a Tourist book is for you.

Greater Than a Tourist- Mackinac Island Michigan USA by Jane Hughes offers the inside scoop on Mackinac Island . Most travel books tell you how to travel like a tourist. Although there is nothing wrong with that, as part of the Greater Than a Tourist series, this book will give you travel tips from someone who has lived at your next travel destination.

In these pages, you will discover advice that will help you throughout your stay. This book will not tell you exact addresses or store hours but instead will give you excitement and knowledge from a local that you may not find in other smaller print travel books.

Travel like a local. Slow down, stay in one place, and get to know the people and the culture. By the time you finish this book, you will be eager and prepared to travel to your next destination.

>TOURIST

TABLE OF CONTENTS

BOOK DESCRIPTION
TABLE OF CONTENTS
ABOUT THE AUTHOR
HOW TO USE THIS BOOK
FROM THE PUBLISHER
OUR STORY
WELCOME TO
> TOURIST
INTRODUCTION

1. Come In Your Walking Shoes
2. Stop And Smell The Roses
3. Don't Sleep In
4. Grab A Coffee
5. Keep Hydrated
6. Dress For The Occasion
7. Leave The Itinerary At Home
8. Find Transportation
9. Have A Camera
10. Chat With The Locals
11. Visit Fort Mackinac
12. Visit Mackinaw Island State Park
13. Visit Fort De Buade
14. Visit Round Island Light
15. Visit Grand Hotel

16. Visit Mackinaw Island Butterfly House
17. Visit Father Marquette National Memorial
18. Visit Haunts Of Mackinaw
19. Visit McGulphin House
20. Visit Bridge View Park
21. Read Up
22. Don't Be Rude
23. Forget Flip Flops
24. Bring A Money Belt, Wallet, Or Crossbody
25. Don't Carry Too Much Cash
26. Get A Tour Guide
27. Don't Judge A Book By It's Cover
28. Don't Sweat The Small Stuff
29. Ferry Rides Are Fun
30. Consider Meal Planning
31. Find Really Cool Souvenirs
32. Bring A Bike
33. Choose A Cool Hotel Note: They're All Cool
34. Ride A Horse
35. Bring Your Pet
36. Go To Sunset Point
37. There Are No Stop Signs
38. Go Wine Tasting
39. Have Breakfast At The Chuckwagon
40. Have An Adventure
41. Don't Go Home Without Fudge

>TOURIST

42. Make Your Way Around The Whole Island
43. Hang Out At Horn's
44. Enjoy The Bridge Walk
45. Last Minute Reminder: Bring Good Shoes
46. Last Minute Reminder: Enjoy The Scenery
47. Last Minute Reminder: Buy Lots Of Fudge
48. Last Minute Reminder: Take A Carriage Ride
49. Last Minute Reminder: Take Pictures
50. Last Minute Reminder: What Are You Waiting For? Book The Trip!

50 THINGS TO KNOW ABOUT PACKING LIGHT FOR TRAVEL

Packing and Planning Tips

Travel Questions

Travel Bucket List

NOTES

ABOUT THE AUTHOR

Jennica Janae is a Self-Publishing Author and personal blogger from southeast, Michigan. She's a strong mixture between Emily Giffin and Jane green.

Aside from her love of writing, Jennica has a very complex love for reading. Her favorite genres include chick lit, science fiction, historical fiction, and classics. She has a dog named Kenzie, she's a slightly trained chef, jokes and sarcasm are pretty much her middle name (huge fan of impractical jokers.)

Jennica love to travel year-round to new and exciting places. She holds a strong love for New York City. One day she hopes to find herself traveling to Australia, Ireland, and the United Kingdom.

HOW TO USE THIS BOOK

The Greater Than a Tourist book series was written by someone who has lived in an area for over three months. The goal of this book is to help travelers either dream or experience different locations by providing opinions from a local. The author has made suggestions based on their own experiences. Please do your own research before traveling to the area in case the suggested places are unavailable.

FROM THE PUBLISHER

Traveling can be one of the most important parts of a person's life. The anticipation and memories that you have are some of the best. As a publisher of the Greater Than a Tourist book series, as well as the popular 50 Things to Know book series, we strive to help you learn about new places, spark your imagination, and inspire you. Wherever you are and whatever you do I wish you safe, fun, and inspiring travel.

Lisa Rusczyk Ed. D.
CZYK Publishing

OUR STORY

Traveling is a passion of the "Greater than a Tourist" series creator. Lisa studied abroad in college, and for their honeymoon Lisa and her husband toured Europe. During her travels to Malta, an older man tried to give her some advice based on his own experience living on the island since he was a young boy. She was not sure if she should talk to the stranger but was interested in his advice. When traveling to some places she was wary to talk to locals because she was afraid that they weren't being genuine. Through her travels, Lisa learned how much locals had to share with tourists. Lisa created the "Greater Than a Tourist" book series to help connect people with locals. A topic that locals are very passionate about sharing.

>TOURIST

WELCOME TO
> TOURIST

>TOURIST

INTRODUCTION

My love for Mackinac Island grew heavily when I first visited the city and island on my fifth grade field trip. It was the first time I'd ever gone anywhere besides my home town. My home town is a super small super quiet place so getting the opportunity to go somewhere new was definitely a thrill for me. But I really didn't know how amazing this place actually was until I experienced it for myself. Although I love this place, I didn't know what I know now, I didn't feel the way about the island that I do today. It is such a warm and special place to visit. I hope you get the opportunity to travel here. I hope you enjoy this place as much as I do, and as much as all of the other fudgies that come here through the year. And I hope you enjoy reading my 50 tips for traveling to Mackinaw, Island!

\> TOURIST

1. COME IN YOUR WALKING SHOES

If there is one thing that I wish someone would have told me my first time going to mackinaw it would be to wear good walking shoes. Walking around on Mackinaw Island is like walking around a theme park. Cedar Point if you will. The island is basically one big giant hill. Good shoes are a must. Having a good sturdy pair of shoes the first time I went as a child would have saved me tons of time whining about the blisters and calluses on my feet.

As much as I sit here and say I have learned from my mistakes, there are times where I clearly haven't and I want to wear the sandals that go with my sundress. My advice is to learn from my mistakes and just come prepared. After all, this is what my book is all about right? I'm here to prepare you for your adventure with advice from my mistake. If I were you I would take it.

2. STOP AND SMELL THE ROSES

All around I'd say that I have a better vacation experience when I take time to smell the roses. By this, I mean leaving work and stress at home enjoying my time here in Mackinaw. I enjoy being in the present moment. This is such a beautiful island, I love stopping and taking in the fairytale scenery. The island is known for its Lilacs. There are Lilac trees all across the island, filling the air with their beautiful floral scent. Every spring, Mackinaw holds the Lilac Festival to celebrate these lovely purple plants. Though I find it best to see and smell them in May or June. But many of them last well into July and August.

3. DON'T SLEEP IN

Who wants to sleep all day on vacation? Not me! I do like to let myself wake up when I wake up when I'm traveling. Which means I don't set an alarm. But I still don't like waking up at noon when I'm somewhere I could be out exploring. I just have to tell myself the night before (if I'm really tired) that I want to get up and have an eventful day and that's what I do. I love waking up early and taking that first step outside, it's like immediate peace washes over me. The island life has me hooked.

4. GRAB A COFFEE

After I've had time to get up and smell the fresh air, I'm headed straight for Lucky Bean Coffee House. Of course, there is a coffee maker in my house there's just something about fresh coffee from a coffee house. Not to mention, they have the best coffee on the island. Lucky bean is where nearly everyone goes to get their morning coffee fix.

5. KEEP HYDRATED

With all of the coffee that lives within my body it's safe to say I drink a lot of water. Being outside on the island or the ferry all day in the hot sun can easily leave me dehydrated. I always, always, always fill up my Tumblr with ice cold water before leaving the house for my adventure of the day.

6. DRESS FOR THE OCCASION

On a hot summer day in Mackinaw I love wearing a nice sun dress and hat. It's the perfect outfit for strolling around the island. That is, if I am just walking or riding in a horse and carriage. In the Summer Mornings are generally cool, with warmer afternoons, so a sweater or hoodie I can put on and take off easily essential. The temperature usually hits an average of about 75 degrees. In the spring the average spring temperatures range between 32 degrees and 47 degrees. Making a jacket or a windbreaker a must. Autumn brings on slightly warmer average temperatures between 47 degrees and 60 degrees. My favorite time of the year here. Now Winters on Mackinac Island can get downright cold. It usually brings lots of snow and ice to the Straits and Lake Huron. I recommend checking out the weather before heading out for a more accurate report.

>TOURIST

7. LEAVE THE ITINERARY AT HOME

I don't mean literally leave your itinerary at home, you might need that. I just hate, hate, hate going on a vacation that is outlined by one of my picky family members. No need to outline every hour of every day, by the minute for each person that's on the trip. I mean, what's the fun in that seriously? When I'm traveling I like to wake up when I wake up, I like to eat when I'm ready to eat. And most important I like to travel the way I want to travel, not the way someone else wants me to. This is a place to explore. This is my place to escape and wonder around aimlessly until I find a cool reenactment to watch. Those things are everywhere here.

8. FIND TRANSPORTATION

One of my absolute favorite things about Mackinaw Island is that they don't drive cars here. Everyone gets around via bike, golf cart, or horse and carriage. I think more places should be like this, the air is so much cleaner. I usually just step outside my door and make my way to an empty carriage.

9. HAVE A CAMERA

I just love taking pictures of the beautiful scenery here. The view of the water and the bridge gets me every time. I also like taking pictures of the battle reenactments, those are pretty neat to look back on too. I recommend having some sort of camera handy, whether it's an instant polaroid or a Canon 1726.

10. CHAT WITH THE LOCALS

I'm only up north during the summer months in Michigan. During the Winter I like to hibernate inside. But when I head north for the summer it's like a fun family reunion. There are quite a few people who are also summer locals on the island. We all like to catch up and share stories about what happened while we were away. Almost like a movie.

"To travel is to live."
— Hans Christian Andersen

>TOURIST

11. VISIT FORT MACKINAC

Fort Mackinac is a former British and American military outpost. The posts was garrisoned from the late 18th century to the late 19th century in on Mackinaw Island I find it a fun place to hang out too! I mean if you think learning about our history is fun, which I do. I really do.

12. VISIT MACKINAW ISLAND STATE PARK

Mackinaw Island state park was established in 1895 as Michigan's first state park. And before that it was known as Mackinac National park, the second national park in the U.S. Something I would have never known if I hadn't went on a tour of the island. That's one of the many reasons I love this place, there is so much history here and we all do a very good job of keeping things the way they are. There's not much change going on here, our history is still very much apart of living on the island today.

13. VISIT FORT DE BUADE

Fort De Buade, the live stage for the French and Indian attacks against Seneca. I love everything about museums. From their history to all the different types such as hands on or galleries. I even love the ones that preserved all the old things that come from our ancestors. For this reason, I think this is a really awesome museum.

14. VISIT ROUND ISLAND LIGHT

Known as the "Old Round Island Point Lighthouse" this is a lighthouse located on the west shore of Round Island. Right in the shipping lanes of the Straits of Mackinac, which connect Lake Michigan and Lake Huron. It's such a beautiful site, especially if you love lighthouses. Which I think everyone loves lighthouses.

>TOURIST

15. VISIT GRAND HOTEL

There were a few times I spent my time on the island in a hotel. Mostly, the Grand Hotel. I believe this is the most immaculate 19th century hotel there is out there. I absolutely love it. I love everything about it from the looks of it, to the view of the water, and even the fun tennis court. Which I sometimes pay to play on. Tennis is the perfect island sport for me. So it makes me even happier that this place has it.

16. VISIT MACKINAW ISLAND BUTTERFLY HOUSE

Butterflies follow me every where I go. Some say this is someone one the other side watching over you and I believe it to be true. I believe it's one of several guardian angels that I have, a different one each and every time. For that reason alone I love the Mackinaw Island Butterfly house. . I always get a ticket as soon as I get on the island because one admission ticket can be used on multiple visits. There are many reasons I love this place like the beauty of it and the learning aspect that comes with it. This place is forever keeping me on my toes.

17. VISIT FATHER MARQUETTE NATIONAL MEMORIAL

I have so much respect for this place, and the thousands of people that gather here each and every year to pay their respects. Father Marquette National Memorial pays tribute to the life and work of Jacques Marquette, French priest and explorer.

18. VISIT HAUNTS OF MACKINAW

I like to think of myself as comedian Sal Vulcano when walking near anything scary. The only difference is that unlike Sal I'm not truly afraid. I live for Halloween. I love dressing up, eating candy, and haunted houses. I was so excited when the island voted on brining more attractions to it for Halloween and they created The Haunts of Mackinaw. Now each year, the whole town gets together for Halloween and numerous locations throughout town gather together to bring Halloween to the island. Ahh, Fall is my favorite time of the year.

>TOURIST

19. VISIT MCGULPHIN HOUSE

As soon as I get off of the ferry and proceed to make my way to my house for the summer one of the first things I pass is the McGulphin House. The McGulphin House is another museum on the island that was built in 1780. Every time I hear someone say it was built in 1780 I just stare in amazement. There's no doubt that it looks as if it was built in 1780. It just makes me think of how far we have come as a country and how people use to live without all of the things that people take for granted these days. I would kill to go back in time and live during a time like this. A time when everything was so technical.

20. VISIT BRIDGE VIEW PARK

I love good park and I love a good view. This place has both of them. I often like to have lunch here and then take pictures for my blog. Really, it's a win win.

> *"Travel makes one modest. You see what a tiny place you occupy in the world."*
> — Gustave Flaubert

21. READ UP

The Town Crier is my go to for information on what's going on, on the island. The people that work there and the paper itself remind me of something you would have seen in Stars Hollow on Gilmore Girls. I live in a small town downstate but nothing compares to the small town feel on the island, especially when it comes to our news.

22. DON'T BE RUDE

I love when I see tourist around town. That's an opportunity for me to make new friends. I love making new friends in new places, that's one of the reasons I love to travel. I feel the same way when new people come into my town. One thing I can't stand though, is when tourist are rude to us locals or disrespectful to our town. It doesn't make them look very good nor do we locals appreciate it. I Personally like to go out of my way to be extra friendly to those I don't know for a couple of reasons. One, I don't know what is going on in someone else's life so I am respectful of that. Two, I guess I was just raised right. I was raised to say please and thank you during every appropriate exchange. I was raised to tip the waiter/waitress good even if I am out of town on a budget. And I was raised to treat others the way I want to be treated plain and simple.

23. FORGET FLIP FLOPS

A friend of mine used to work for an airline and she would always told me never to wear sandals on board an aircraft. In the unlikely event of an emergency a good pair of sturdy shoes will protect my feet from heat or sharp objects. Although when I'm not flying into northern, Mi I find it best to leave the flip flops at home. When I live on the island I spend majority of my time walking or riding a bike so I like to keep my feet comfortable and clean. As I often like to say: Comfort over cuteness.

24. BRING A MONEY BELT, WALLET, OR CROSSBODY

If I get mugged I can calmly hand over the wallet and carry on with my life in the unlikely event of this happening. Or   if I plan to do pretty much any activity there is on the island I find it best that I don't carry around my huge Fossil tote. I try to be as minimal as possible when exploring in Mackinaw. I never know what kind of adventure I could get into.

25. DON'T CARRY TOO MUCH CASH

I can't remember visiting a country in the last 10 years that doesn't have ATMs, so there's really no need to carry about more cash than I need for the day. I have a travel fireproof safe that goes with my nearly every where I go that's where I store all of my money. If I need some I only carry around a little bit, if any really. Most these days places have some kind of card or chip reader. Or like I said a nearby ATM. I try to just keep it simple.

26. GET A TOUR GUIDE

When visiting cultural monuments, I always take the offer of a local guide. This helps me open my eyes to so much more. More than if I try and do it alone with a guide book. Don't get me wrong a simple map and a good written guide book can do wonders. Maybe I just think it's all apart of the experience. I

>TOURIST

love enjoying every aspect of every new experience that I get the opportunity to partake in. This is why I love Mackinaw Island Carriage Tours. They offer engaging tours of the whole island.

27. DON'T JUDGE A BOOK BY IT'S COVER

Just because a person is Caucasian, doesn't mean that person speaks English. I come across people from many different parts of the world traveling to mackinaw each year. I've met people from the Netherlands, people from Ireland, and people from Australia. I still think it's crazy. I never would have though that something so close to were I grew up (in a sense) , would be such a cool place for people to travel to . And for people to do it as often as they do amazes me. I love it. Being in such a diverse place is a good way to learn and accept the habits of people from other cultures. Recognizing that we're all the same. It's a beautiful thing.

28. DON'T SWEAT THE SMALL STUFF

I without a doubt, always get some sort of anxiety when I travel. I'm not quite sure why as it's my favorite thing to do. But I do. I know that traveling can be frustrating at times. And unexpected uncirmunstantial things can happen. Deep down inside I don't like to sweat the small stuff. I like to have an open mind, especially when traveling.

29. FERRY RIDES ARE FUN

For most of us Mackinac Island locals, we know that the ferry is a necessary means of transportation to and from the island. What most people don't emphasize, however, is that the ferry itself is a form of entertainment. The ferry offers a 20 minute ride with incredible views of Lake Huron, the Mackinac Bridge, light houses, sailboats, and Mackinac Island mansions. I like to Grab a spot on the upper deck on my way over. On the Ferry the ship's crew provides information about the ferry and Mackinac Island. If I find yourself riding the ferry back at night for a sunset cruise, I sit inside the lower cabin. This helps me stay warm when the becomes chillier.

30. CONSIDER MEAL PLANNING

There are several great restaurants to choose from on Mackinac Island. With cuisine that ranges from hamburgers to high-end dinners. Mackinaw island is however a very popular island. I always make sure I get to my favorite dinner restaurant early to beat crowds, or consider switching things up with a picnic by the water (particularly, Bridge View Park.) There's so much beauty there, you won't even miss the table and chairs. But no matter what I find it easy to plan which times through the day I'm going to either dine in or dine out. That way I beat the rush.

> *"As the traveler who has once been from home is wiser than he who has never left his own doorstep, so a knowledge of one other culture should sharpen our ability to scrutinize more steadily, to appreciate more lovingly, our own."*
> – Margaret Mead

31. FIND REALLY COOL SOUVENIRS

I just adore souvenir shopping. The problem with souvenirs, however, is that they can sometimes be a little tacky. Never fear! Mackinac Island has plenty of little boutiques and galleries where you can find something that's both useful and out of the norm. My families favorite is Little Luxuries of Mackinac Island. Here pretty pillows, stationery, and kitchen products set the scene. A lot of the items in this store are made by local artists. So I can shop small and support local business at the same time. And I do love to support local and small businesses. I should really start to advocate for them more often.

32. BRING A BIKE

I strongly advise in bringing a bike to the island if applicable. There are no cars allowed on Mackinac Island, so biking is a lifesaver when getting from point A to point B quickly. Plus, there are so many gorgeous views to take in on Mackinac Island's own bike tour.

>TOURIST

Keep In Mind:

Ferries may charge an additional fee for you to bring your bike with you (Price subject to change) so be sure to factor that in to your planning. Another option is to rent a bike on the island. There are several places on the island where you can rent bikes by the hour or day, so depending on your needs, you can pick one up when you get there.

33. CHOOSE A COOL HOTEL NOTE: THEY'RE ALL COOL

One of the biggest decisions I always had to make before becoming a local on the island was always deciding on where to stay. It wasn't because the lack of options, there is a variety. It was because my options were so unbelievably cool. I mean it. The hotels are beautiful here.

34. RIDE A HORSE

Normally, not having a car would be considered a huge inconvenience. I for one, would hate to be without a car twenty-four seven. Although it's definitely a privilege to be able to take time away from that luxury I don't think I could do it for good. On Mackinac, the absence of cars provides a calm and pleasant atmosphere. Getting around here is no trouble because all of the restaurants and shops throughout town are in a compacted area and are easy to get to. But the best thing about the island is the presence of horses that only adds to the calm atmosphere. You can either call a carriage to pick you up or just climb up into an open one like a cab. There are also a number of horse stables where you can go if you want to take a tour of the island on horseback. Which I highly recommend!

35. BRING YOUR PET

The island is a very pet friendly environment. In fact pets can stay for free at Mission Point Resort. I know a lot of hotels around the world charge extra for your pet to stay with you so I thought that was cool to learn. Mission Point is such a nice resort too. It sits right on the shore of the jewels of the Great Lakes.

>TOURIST

36. GO TO SUNSET POINT

There's a well-kept secret on the island that very few know about. Hidden behind the Inn at Stonecliffe there is a beautiful view of the sunset. We call it Sunset Point. In my well thought out imagination this is the perfect proposal spot for just about anybody. When you walk your future finance out there and show them the view of the beautiful orange and yellow sky that's blends perfectly without any clouds. Pointing to the sky for them to look while you kneel down behind them waiting for them to turn around be caught by surprise. Caught by surprise, their eyes begin to fill with tears of happiness. After just a moment of silence you begin to worry, then it all fades away when they realize they haven't said anything and softly say "yes!"

37. THERE ARE NO STOP SIGNS

There actually aren't really any street signs that pertain to driving a vehicle. The reasoning for that probably being that there little to no vehicle's on the island. Now there are vehicle's there for emergency situations, there has to be. But other than that we get around just find on foot, by bike, or by horse. Just like they did in the good ole days. And we can breathe just fine too, those of us that don't smoke cigarettes that is. This being said, I'm always extra careful when cross the street. If you're not worried about this seeing as there aren't any cars around, you clearly have never been trampled by an upset horse. I have, therefore I look before I cross.

38. GO WINE TASTING

The really awesome resort that offers free room and board for furry family members also offers wine tasting. I just love wine tasting. Actually, I love anything about wine. It's life to me, next to coffee. And no I'm not dependent on it. I just enjoy it, especially while on the island.

39. HAVE BREAKFAST AT THE CHUCKWAGON

This is the absolute best place to have breakfast on the entire island. Breakfast is my favorite time of the day. I love everything about it. From the fresh coffee brewing to the morning paper and even the selection of food that we as humans put into this category. Since it is the most important meal of the day it's imperative to do it right. That includes eating at the right restaurant.

40. HAVE AN ADVENTURE

Having a nightcap at the Cupola Bar at the Grand Hotel is a good way to meet other tourist/locals while all while having a ball. I often enjoy a million dollar view while sipping a cocktail or glass of champagne while I'm there. I've learned that his is the perfect way for me to step out of my comfort zone and into vacation mode. On that note, the Grand Hotel does not charge a fee for entering in the evening.

> *"Nobody can discover the world for somebody else. Only when we discover it for ourselves does it become common ground and a common bond and we cease to be alone."*
> – Wendell Berry

41. DON'T GO HOME WITHOUT FUDGE

Growing up, I don't recall a time when we didn't have to make sure and stop by JoAnn's and grab a few pounds of fudge to bring home. Mom either knew we were all going to want some during the weeks to come or we had to get some for my grandparents. I particularly remember always buying peanut butter, that was my grandparents favorite. I happen to believe this was the cause for the sweet tooth I know have as soon as I get to the island, but I'm not complaining. And I never go home without fudge. There's a reason we call our tourist fudgies.

42. MAKE YOUR WAY AROUND THE WHOLE ISLAND

Since I live in such a beautiful place, I find it imperative to explore all aspects of it when I get the chance. Normally, I don't know what I want to do when I get to my destination. I'll usually arrive and spend a little bit of time on google maps using the google street view (which is conveniently what it's made for). If I do this I get a quick peak at the destination from the streets and landmarks giving me an opportunity to plan my route better.

43. HANG OUT AT HORN'S

In my life, having a wild Taco Tuesday is good way to get some excitement flowing in the air. Since the island has a very different type of environment than I live in, in Southeast, Mi. I have to adapt myself accordingly. When I discovered Horn's Bar and Grill I was almost immediately hooked. They have the best Mexican and margarita' on the island.

44. ENJOY THE BRIDGE WALK

Traveling over labor day weekend allows the opportunity to gather in the annual Mackinaw Island Bridge walk with tens of thousands of people. Starting in St. Ignace the walk is roughly a five mile trek across the Mackinac Bridge that connects the lower and upper peninsulas of Michigan.

45. LAST MINUTE REMINDER: BRING GOOD SHOES

I cannot seem to stress the importance of having good shoes on the island enough. This is most likely my subconscious talking to the inner child in me that wants to wear my jeweled sandals simply because they match my outfit. I couldn't bear to wear shoes that don't match. As I've gotten older I've realized the important proper body mechanics like having the right posture, stretching, lifting with your lower half instead of your upper half. And even wearing the proper shoes around an island that is made of hills and bike riding.

46. LAST MINUTE REMINDER: ENJOY THE SCENERY

As a tourist the main thing that attracts me to a specific locations is usually the scenery. How the place looks on the brochure. When I arrive to the place I want to make sure that it lives up the expectations that I set when I looked into the trip. 9.10 that is the case. The only way I can seem to determine if it really lives up to my expectations is to

>TOURIST

really stop and take it all in. I look around for the unique beauty of the place.

47. LAST MINUTE REMINDER: BUY LOTS OF FUDGE

Like I said, we call our tourist fudgies for a reason. The island literally has the best fudge around. And there's like every flavor ever made in fudge form. I am more of a chocolate peanut butter gal myself, but there is definitely a fudge for everyone out there.

48. LAST MINUTE REMINDER: TAKE A CARRIAGE RIDE

Since there are no cars that means there are only a couple of options left. If you're still here with me then you know what they are already. Golf cart, bike, or horse. It's a wonderful thing to experience when you come to Mackinaw if applicable. Riding in a horse and carriage helps to complete the overall experience of coming to Mackinaw island.

49. LAST MINUTE REMINDER: TAKE PICTURES

Pictures are simply physical memories. Having a photographic memory is great, but having a picture to stare at is even better. Pictures are great for decorating houses with or even making scrap books. I always like to take at least one picture every where I go. I'll admit I've been so distracted on vacation that I completely ignored every and all technology thus forgetting to take a picture. But once I realized that I missed the opportunity to take a picture it made me slightly sad. As much as I love to travel I 'm not rich by any means. And this means, who knows when I'll get the opportunity to go back to that place. That's a huge reason I love taking pictures when I travel, to capture that memory for as long as I live. I recommend you do that too.

50. LAST MINUTE REMINDER: WHAT ARE YOU WAITING FOR? BOOK THE TRIP!

I know what you're thinking, this place sounds awesome! And the truth is, it is awesome. Mackinaw island is an awesome place to visit. It's one of the

>TOURIST

most beautiful islands you will ever set your eyes on. It's the best place to take a family vacation. It's a place of calmness. It's a place you can learn. It's a place you can propose. It's so many wonderful things. I even begin to express all of there reasons this is one of the best islands in the county. One thing I will say is that it definitely speaks for itself.

\>TOURIST

BONUS BOOK

50 THINGS TO KNOW ABOUT PACKING LIGHT FOR TRAVEL

PACK THE RIGHT WAY EVERY TIME

AUTHOR: MANIDIPA BHATTACHARYYA

First Published in 2015 by Dr. Lisa Rusczyk. Copyright 2015. All Rights Reserved. No part of this publication may be reproduced, including scanning and photocopying, or distributed in any form or by any means, electronic or mechanical, or stored in a database or retrieval system without prior written permission from the publisher.

Disclaimer: The publisher has put forth an effort in preparing and arranging this book. The information provided herein by the author is provided "as is". Use this information at your own risk. The publisher is not a licensed doctor. Consult your doctor before engaging in any medical activities. The publisher and author disclaim any liabilities for any loss of profit or commercial or personal damages resulting from the information contained in this book.

Edited by Melanie Howthorne

ABOUT THE AUTHOR

Manidipa Bhattacharyya is a creative writer and editor, with an education in English literature and Linguistics. After working in the IT industry for seven long years she decided to call it quits and follow her heart instead. Manidipa has been ghost writing, editing, proof reading and doing secondary research services for many story tellers and article writers for about three years. She stays in Kolkata, India with her husband and a busy two year old. In her own time Manidipa enjoys travelling, photography and writing flash fiction.

Manidipa believes in travelling light and never carries anything that she couldn't haul herself on a trip. However, travelling with her child changed the scenario. She seemed to carry the entire world with her for the baby on the first two trips. But good sense prevailed and she is again working her way to becoming a light traveler, this time with a kid.

>TOURIST

INTRODUCTION

*He who would travel happily
must travel light.*

-Antoine de Saint-Exupéry

Travel takes you to different places from seas and mountains to deserts and much more. In your travels you get to interact with different people and their cultures. You will, however, enjoy the sights and interact positively with these new people even more, if you are travelling light.

When you travel light your mind can be free from worry about your belongings. You do not have to spend precious vacation time waiting for your luggage to arrive after a long flight. There is be no chance of your bags going missing and the best part is that you need not pay a fee for checked baggage.

People who have mastered this art of packing light will root for you to take only one carry-on, wherever you go. However, many people can find it really hard to pack light. More so if you are travelling with children. Differentiating between "must have" and "just in case" items is the starting point. There will be ample shopping avenues at your destination which are just waiting to be explored.

This book will show you 'packing' in a new 'light' – pun intended – and help you to embrace light packing practices for all of your future travels.

Off to packing!

DEDICATION

I dedicate this book to all the travel buffs that I know, who have given me great insights into the contents of their backpacks.

THE RIGHT TRAVEL GEAR

1. CHOOSE YOUR TRAVEL GEAR CAREFULLY

While selecting your travel gear, pick items that are light weight, durable and most importantly, easy to carry. There are cases with wheels so you can drag them along – these are usually on the heavy side because of the trolley. Alternatively a backpack that you can carry comfortably on your back, or even a duffel bag that you can carry easily by hand or sling across your body are also great options. Whatever you choose, one thing to keep in mind is that the luggage itself should not weigh a ton, this will give you the flexibility to bring along one extra pair of shoes if you so desire.

>TOURIST

2. CARRY THE MINIMUM NUMBER OF BAGS

Selecting light weight luggage is not everything. You need to restrict the number of bags you carry as well. One carry-on size bag is ideal for light travel. Most carriers allow one cabin baggage plus one purse, handbag or camera bag as long as it slides under the seat in front. So technically, you can carry two items of luggage without checking them in.

3. PACK ONE EXTRA BAG

Always pack one extra empty bag along with your essential items. This could be a very light weight duffel bag or even a sturdy tote bag which takes up minimal space. In the event that you end up buying a lot of souvenirs, you already have a handy bag to stuff all that into and do not have to spend time hunting for an appropriate bag.

> *I'm very strict with my packing and have everything in its right place. I never change a rule. I hardly use anything in the hotel room. I wheel my own wardrobe in and that's it.*

Charlie Watts

CLOTHES & ACCESSORIES

4. PLAN AHEAD

Figure out in advance what you plan to do on your trip. That will help you to pick that one dress you need for the occasion. If you are going to attend a wedding then you have to carry formal wear. If not, you can ditch the gown for something lighter that will be comfortable during long walks or on the beach.

5. WEAR THAT JACKET

Remember that wearing items will not add extra luggage for your air travel. So wear that bulky jacket that you plan to carry for your trip. This saves space and can also help keep you warm during the chilly flight.

6. MIX AND MATCH

Carry clothes that can be interchangeably used to reinvent your look. Find one top that goes well with a couple of pairs of pants or skirts. Use tops, shirts and jackets wisely along with other accessories like a scarf or a stole to create a new look.

\>TOURIST

7. CHOOSE YOUR FABRIC WISELY

Stuffing clothes in cramped bags definitely takes its toll which results in wrinkles. It is best to carry wrinkle free, synthetic clothes or merino tops. This will eliminate the need for that small iron you usually bring along.

8. DITCH CLOTHES PACK UNDERWEAR

Pack more underwear and socks. These are the things that will give you a fresh feel even if you do not get a chance to wear fresh clothes. Moreover these are easy to wash and can be dried inside the hotel room itself.

9. CHOOSE DARK OVER LIGHT

While picking your clothes choose dark coloured ones. They are easy to colour coordinate and can last longer before needing a wash. Accidental food spills and dirt from the road are less visible on darker clothes.

10. WEAR YOUR JEANS

Take only one pair of Jeans with you, which you should wear on the flight. Remember to pick a pair that can be worn for sightseeing trips and is equally eloquent for dinner. You can add variety by adding light weight cargoes and chinos.

11. CARRY SMART ACCESSORIES

The right accessory can give you a fresh look even with the same old dress. An intelligent neck-piece, a couple of bright scarves, stoles or a sarong can be used in a number of ways to add variety to your clothing. These light weight beauties can double up as a nursing cover, a light blanket, beach wear, a modesty cover for visiting places of worship, and also makes for an enthralling game of peek-a-boo.

12. LEARN TO FOLD YOUR GARMENTS

Seasoned travellers all swear by rolling their clothes for compact and wrinkle free packing. Bundle packing, where you roll the clothes around a central object as if tying it up, is also a popular method of compact and wrinkle free packing. Stacking folded clothes one on top of another is a big no-no as it makes creases extreme and they are difficult to get rid of without ironing.

>TOURIST

13. WASH YOUR DIRTY LAUNDRY

One of the ways to avoid carrying loads of clothes is to wash the clothes you carry. At some places you might get to use the laundry services or a Laundromat but if you are in a pinch, best solution is to wash them yourself. If that is the plan then carrying quick drying clothes is highly recommended, which most often also happen to be the wrinkle free variety.

14. LEAVE THOSE TOWELS BEHIND

Regular towels take up a lot of space, are heavy and take ages to dry out. If you are staying at hotels they will provide you with towels anyway. If you are travelling to a remote place, where the availability of towels look doubtful, carry a light weight travel towel of viscose material to do the job.

15. USE A COMPRESSION BAG

Compression bags are getting lots of recommendation now days from regular travellers. These are useful for saving space in your luggage when you have to pack bulky dresses. While packing for the return trip, get help from the hotel staff to arrange a vacuum cleaner.

FOOTWEAR

16. PUT ON YOUR HIKING BOOTS

If you have plans to go hiking or trekking during your trip, you will need those bulky hiking boots. The best way to carry them is to wear them on flight to save space and luggage weight. You can remove the boots once inside and be comfortable in your socks.

17. PICKING THE RIGHT SHOES

Shoes are often the bulkiest items, along with being the dainty if you are a female. They need care and take up a lot of space in your luggage. It is advisable therefore to pick shoes very carefully. If you plan to do a lot of walking and site seeing, then wearing a pair of comfortable walking shoes are a must. For more formal occasions you can carry durable, light weight flats which will not take up much space.

18. STUFF SHOES

If you happen to pack a pair of shoes, ensure you utilize their hollow insides. Tuck small items like rolled up socks or belts to save space. They will also be easy to find.

TOILETRIES

19. STASHING TOILETRIES

Carry only absolute necessities. Airline rules dictate that for one carry-on bag, liquids and gels must be in 3.4 ounce (100ml) bottles or less, and must be packed in a one quart zip-lock bag. If you are planning to stay in a hotel, the basic things will be provided for you. It's best is to buy the rest from the local market at your destination.

20. TAKE ALONG TAMPONS

Tampons are a hard to find item in a lot of countries. Figure out how many you need and pack accordingly. For longer stays you can buy them online and have them delivered to where you are staying.

21. GET PAMPERED BEFORE YOU TRAVEL

Some avid travellers suggest getting a pedicure and manicure just the day before travelling. This not only gives you a well kept look, you also save the trouble of packing nail polish. Remember, every little bit of weight reduced adds up.

ELECTRONICS

22. LUGGING ALONG ELECTRONICS

Electronics have a large role to play in our lives today. Most of us cannot imagine our lives away from our phones, laptops or tablets. However while travelling, one must consider the amount of weight these electronics add to our luggage. Thankfully smart phones come along with all the essentials tools like a camera, email access, picture editing tools and more. They are smart to the point of eliminating the need to carry multiple gadgets. Choose a smart phone that suits all your requirements and travel with the world in your palms or pocket.

23. REDUCE THE NUMBER OF CHARGERS

If you do travel with multiple electronic devices, you will have to bear the additional burden of carrying all their chargers too. Check if a single charger can be used for multiple devices. You might also consider investing in a pocket charger. These small devices support multiple devices while keeping you charged on the go.

\>TOURIST

24. TRAVEL FRIENDLY APPS

Along with smart phones come numerous apps, which are immensely helpful in our travels. You name it and you have an app for it at hand – take pictures, sharing with friends and family, torch to light dark roads, maps, checking flight/train times, find hotels and many other things. Use these smart alternatives to traditional items like books to eliminate weight and save space.

> *I get ideas about what's essential when packing my suitcase.*

-Diane von Furstenberg

TRAVELLING WITH KIDS

25. BRING ALONG THE STROLLER

Kids might enjoy walking for a while but they soon tire out and a stroller is the just the right thing for them to rest in while you continue your tour. Strollers also double duty as a luggage carrier and shopping bag holder. Remember to pick a light weight, easy to handle brand of stroller. Better yet, find out in advance if you can rent a stroller at your destination.

26. BRING ONLY ENOUGH DIAPERS FOR YOUR TRIP

Diapers take up a lot of space and add to the weight of your luggage. Therefore it is advisable to carry just enough diapers to last through the trip and a few for afterwards, till you buy fresh stock at your destination. Unless of course you are travelling to a really remote area, in which case you have no choice but to carry the load. Otherwise diapers are something you will find pretty easily.

27. TAKE ONLY A COUPLE OF TOYS

Children are easily attracted by new things in their environment. While travelling they will find numerous 'new' objects to scrutinize and play with. Packing just one favorite toy is enough, or if there is no favorite toy leave out all of them in favor of stories or imaginary games.

28. CARRY KID FRIENDLY SNACKS

Create a small snack counter in your bag to store away quick bites for those sudden hunger pangs. Depending on the child's age this could include chocolates, raisins, dry fruits, granola bars or biscuits. Also keep a bottle of water handy for your little one.

These things do not add much weight and can be adjusted in a handbag or knapsack.

29. GAMES TO CARRY

Create some travel specific, imaginary games if you have slightly grown up children, like spot the attractions. Keep a coloring book and colors handy for in-flight or hotel time. Apps on your smart phone can keep the children engaged with cartoons and story books. Older children are often entertained by games available on phones or tablets. This cuts the weight of luggage down while keeping the kids entertained.

30. LET THE KIDS CARRY THEIR LOAD

A good thing is to start early sharing of responsibilities. Let your child pick a bag of his or her choice and pack it themselves. Keep tabs on what they are stuffing in their bags by asking if they will be using that item on the trip. It could start out being just an entertainment bag initially but with growing years they will learn to sort the useful from the superfluous. Children as little as four can maneuver a small trolley suitcase like a pro- their experience in pull along toys credit. If you are worried that you may be pulling it for them, you may want to start with a backpack.

31. DECIDE ON LOCATION FOR CHILDREN TO SLEEP

While on a trip you might not always get a crib at your destination, and carrying one will make life all the more difficult. Instead call ahead to see if there are any cribs or roll out beds for children. You may even put blankets on the floor. Weave them a story about camping and they will gladly sleep without any trouble.

32. GET BABY PRODUCTS DELIVERED AT YOUR DESTINATION

If you are absolutely paranoid about not getting your favourite variety of diaper or brand of baby food, check out online stores like amazon.com for services in your destination city. You can buy things online ahead of your travel and get them delivered to your hotel upon arrival.

33. FEEDING NEEDS OF YOUR INFANTS

If you are travelling with a breastfed infant, you save the trouble of carrying bottles and bottle sanitization kits. For special food, or medications, you may need to call ahead to make sure you have a refrigerator where you are staying.

34. FEEDING NEEDS OF YOUR TODDLER

With the progression from infancy to toddler, their dietary requirements too evolve. You will have to pack some snacks for travelling time. Fresh fruits and vegetables can be purchased at your destination. Most of the cities you travel to in whichever part of the world, will have baby food products and formulas, available at the local drug-store or the supermarket.

35. PICKING CLOTHES FOR YOUR BABY

Contrary to popular belief, babies can do without many changes of clothes. At the most pack 2 outfits per day. Pack mix and match type clothes for your little one as well. Pick things which are comfortable to wear and quick to dry.

36. SELECTING SHOES FOR YOUR BABY

Like outfits, kids can make do with two pairs of comfortable shoes. If you can get some water resistant shoes it will be best. To expedite drying wet shoes, you can stuff newspaper in them then wrap them with newspaper and leave them to dry overnight.

37. KEEP ONE CHANGE OF CLOTHES HANDY

Travelling with kids can be tricky. Keep a change of clothes for the kids and mum handy in your purse or tote bag. This takes a bit of space in your hand luggage but comes extremely handy in case there are any accidents or spills.

38. LEAVE BEHIND BABY ACCESSORIES

Baby accessories like their bed, bath tub, car seat, crib etc. should be left at home. Many hotels provide a crib on request, while car seats can be borrowed from friends or rented. Babies can be given a bath in the hotel sink or even in the adult bath tub with a little bit of water. If you bring a few bath toys, they can be used in the bath, pool, and out of water. They can also be sanitized easily in the sink.

39. CARRY A SMALL LOAD OF PLASTIC BAGS

With children around there are chances of a number of soiled clothes and diapers. These plastic bags help to sort the dirt from the clean inside your big bag.

These are very light weight and come in handy to other carry stuff as well at times.

PACK WITH A PURPOSE

40. PACKING FOR BUSINESS TRIPS

One neutral-colored suit should suffice. It can be paired with different shirts, ties and accessories for different occasions. One pair of black suit pants could be worn with a matching jacket for the office or with a snazzy top for dinner.

41. PACKING FOR A CRUISE

Most cruises have formal dinners, and that formal dress usually takes up a lot of space. However you might find a tuxedo to rent. For women, a short black dress with multiple accessory options will do the trick.

42. PACKING FOR A LONG TRIP OVER DIFFERENT CLIMATES

The secret packing mantra for travel over multiple climates is layering. Layering traps air around your body creating insulation against the cold. The same light t-shirt that is comfortable in a warmer climate can be the innermost layer in a colder climate.

REDUCE SOME MORE WEIGHT

43. LEAVE PRECIOUS THINGS AT HOME

Things that you would hate to lose or get damaged leave them at home. Precious jewelry, expensive gadgets or dresses, could be anything. You will not require these on your trip. Leave them at home and spare the load on your mind.

44. SEND SOUVENIRS BY MAIL

If you have spent all your money on purchasing souvenirs, carrying them back in the same bag that you brought along would be difficult. Either pack everything in another bag and check it in the airport or get everything shipped to your home. Use an international carrier for a secure transit, but this could be more expensive than the checking fees at the airport.

45. AVOID CARRYING BOOKS

Books equal to weight. There are many reading apps which you can download on your smart phone or tab.

Plus there are gadgets like Kindle and Nook that are thinner and lighter alternatives to your regular book.

CHECK, GET, SET, CHECK AGAIN

46. STRATEGIZE BEFORE PACKING

Create a travel list and prepare all that you think you need to carry along. Keep everything on your bed or floor before packing and then think through once again – do I really need that? Any item that meets this question can be avoided. Remove whatever you don't really need and pack the rest.

47. TEST YOUR LUGGAGE

Once you have fully packed for the trip take a test trip with your luggage. Take your bags and go to town for window shopping for an hour. If you enjoy your hour long trip it is good to go, if not, go home and reduce the load some more. Repeat this test till you hit the right weight.

48. ADD A ROLL OF DUCT TAPE

You might wonder why, when this book has been talking about reducing stuff, we're suddenly asking you to pack something totally unusual. This is because when you have limited supplies, duct tape is immensely helpful for small repairs – a broken bag, leaking zip-lock bag, broken sunglasses, you name it and duct tape can fix it, temporarily.

49. LIST OF ESSENTIAL ITEMS

Even though the emphasis is on packing light, there are things which have to be carried for any trip. Here is our list of essentials:

- Passport/Visa or any other ID

- Any other paper work that might be required on a trip like permits, hotel reservation confirmations etc.

- Medicines – all your prescription medicines and emergency kit, especially if you are travelling with children

- Medical or vaccination records

- Money in foreign currency if travelling to a different country

- Tickets- Email or Message them to your phone

>TOURIST

50. MAKE THE MOST OF YOUR TRIP

Wherever you are going, whatever you hope to do we encourage you to embrace it whole-heartedly. Take in the scenery, the culture and above all, enjoy your time away from home.

> *On a long journey even a straw weighs heavy.*

-Spanish Proverb

>TOURIST

PACKING AND PLANNING TIPS

A Week before Leaving

- Arrange for someone to take care of pets and water plants.
- Stop mail and newspaper.
- Notify Credit Card companies where you are going.
- Change your thermostat settings.
- Car inspected, oil is changed, and tires have the correct pressure.
- Passports and photo identification is up to date.
- Pay bills.
- Copy important items and download travel Apps.
- Start collecting small bills for tips.

Right Before Leaving

- Clean out refrigerator.
- Empty garbage cans.
- Lock windows.
- Make sure you have the proper identification with you.
- Bring cash for tips.
- Remember travel documents.
- Lock door behind you.
- Remember wallet.
- Unplug items in house and pack chargers.

>TOURIST

READ OTHER GREATER THAN A TOURIST BOOKS

Greater Than a Tourist San Miguel de Allende Guanajuato Mexico: 50 Travel Tips from a Local by Tom Peterson

Greater Than a Tourist – Lake George Area New York USA: 50 Travel Tips from a Local by Janine Hirschklau

Greater Than a Tourist – Monterey California United States: 50 Travel Tips from a Local by Katie Begley

Greater Than a Tourist – Chanai Crete Greece: 50 Travel Tips from a Local by Dimitra Papagrigoraki

Greater Than a Tourist – The Garden Route Western Cape Province South Africa: 50 Travel Tips from a Local by Li-Anne McGregor van Aardt

Greater Than a Tourist – Sevilla Andalusia Spain: 50 Travel Tips from a Local by Gabi Gazon

Greater Than a Tourist – Kota Bharu Kelantan Malaysia: 50 Travel Tips from a Local by Aditi Shukla

Children's Book: Charlie the Cavalier Travels the World by Lisa Rusczyk

>TOURIST

> TOURIST

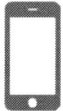

Visit Greater Than a Tourist for Free Travel Tips
http://GreaterThanATourist.com

Sign up for the Greater Than a Tourist Newsletter for discount days, new books, and travel information:
http://eepurl.com/cxspyf

Follow us on Facebook for tips, images, and ideas:
https://www.facebook.com/GreaterThanATourist

Follow us on Pinterest for travel tips and ideas:
http://pinterest.com/GreaterThanATourist

Follow us on Instagram for beautiful travel images:
http://Instagram.com/GreaterThanATourist

>TOURIST

> TOURIST

Please leave your honest review of this book on Amazon and Goodreads. Please send your feedback to GreaterThanaTourist@gmail.com as we continue to improve the series. We appreciate your positive and constructive feedback. Thank you.

>TOURIST

METRIC CONVERSIONS

TEMPERATURE

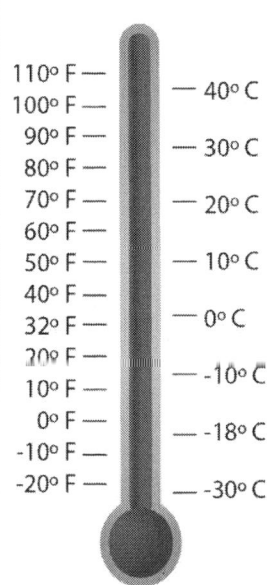

110° F — 40° C
100° F
90° F — 30° C
80° F
70° F — 20° C
60° F
50° F — 10° C
40° F
32° F — 0° C
20° F
10° F — -10° C
0° F
-10° F — -18° C
-20° F — -30° C

To convert F to C:

Subtract 32, and then multiply by 5/9 or .5555.

To Convert C to F:
Multiply by 1.8
and then add 32.

32F = 0C

LIQUID VOLUME

To Convert:.................Multiply by
U.S. Gallons to Liters.............. 3.8
U.S. Liters to Gallons 26
Imperial Gallons to U.S. Gallons 1.2
Imperial Gallons to Liters....... 4.55
Liters to Imperial Gallons 22
1 Liter = .26 U.S. Gallon
1 U.S. Gallon = 3.8 Liters

DISTANCE

To convert ....Multiply by
Inches to Centimeters ...2.54
Centimeters to Inches 39
Feet to Meters........................3
Meters to Feet 3.28
Yards to Meters 91
Meters to Yards 1.09
Miles to Kilometers 1.61
Kilometers to Miles............. .62
1 Mile = 1.6 km
1 km = .62 Miles

WEIGHT

1 Ounce = .28 Grams
1 Pound = .4555 Kilograms
1 Gram = .04 Ounce
1 Kilogram = 2.2 Pounds

\>TOURIST

TRAVEL QUESTIONS

- Do you bring presents home to family or friends after a vacation?
- Do you get motion sick?
- Do you have a favorite billboard?
- Do you know what to do if there is a flat tire?
- Do you like a sun roof open?
- Do you like to eat in the car?
- Do you like to wear sun glasses in the car?
- Do you like toppings on your ice cream?
- Do you use public bathrooms?
- Did you bring your cell phone and does it have power?
- Do you have a form of identification with you?
- Have you ever been pulled over by a cop?
- Have you ever given money to a stranger on a road trip?
- Have you ever taken a road trip with animals?
- Have you ever went on a vacation alone?
- Have you ever run out of gas?

- If you could move to any place in the world, where would it be?
- If you could travel anywhere in the world, where would you travel?
- If you could travel in any vehicle, which one would it be?
- If you had three things to wish for from a magic genie, what would they be?
- If you have a driver's license, how many times did it take you to pass the test?
- What are you the most afraid of on vacation?
- What do you want to get away from the most when you are on vacation?
- What foods smells bad to you?
- What item do you bring on ever trip with you away from home?
- What makes you sleepy?
- What song would you love to hear on the radio when you're cruising on the highway?
- What travel job would you want the least?
- What will you miss most while you are away from home?
- What is something you always wanted to try?

\>TOURIST

- What is the best road side attraction that you ever saw?
- What is the farthest distance you ever biked?
- What is the farthest distance you ever walked?
- What is the weirdest thing you needed to buy while on vacation?
- What is your favorite candy?
- What is your favorite color car?
- What is your favorite family vacation?
- What is your favorite food?
- What is your favorite gas station drink or food?
- What is your favorite license plate design?
- What is your favorite restaurant?
- What is your favorite smell?
- What is your favorite song?
- What is your favorite sound that nature makes?
- What is your favorite thing to bring home from a vacation?
- What is your favorite vacation with friends?
- What is your favorite way to relax?

- What is your favorite weather conditions while driving?
- Where is the farthest place you ever traveled in a car?
- Where is the farthest place you ever went North, South, East and West?
- Where is your favorite place in the world?
- Who is your favorite singer?
- Who taught you how to drive?
- Who will you miss the most while you are away?
- Who if the first person you will contact when you get to your destination?
- Who brought you on your first vacation?
- Who likes to travel the most in your life?
- Would you rather be hot or cold?
- Would you rather drive above, below, or at the speed limited?
- Would you rather drive on a highway or a back road?
- Would you rather go on a train or a boat?
- Would you rather go to the beach or the woods?

>TOURIST

TRAVEL BUCKET LIST

1.

2.

3.

4.

5.

6.

7.

8.

9.

10.

>TOURIST NOTES

Made in the USA
Middletown, DE
27 August 2022